HAL•LEONARD INSTRUMENTAL PLAY-ALONG

AUDIO ACCESS INCLUDED

PLAYBACK+
Speed • Pitch • Balance • Loop

KEYBOARD PERCUSSION

Simple Songs

T0084976

2 .... All of Me

3 .... Can You Feel the Love Tonight

4 .... Can't Help Falling in Love

5 .... Evermore

6 .... Hallelujah

7 .... Happy

8 .... Hey, Soul Sister

9 .... I Gotta Feeling

10 .... I'm Yours

11 .... Lava

12 .... My Heart Will Go On
(Love Theme from "Titanic")

13 .... Rolling in the Deep

14 .... Viva La Vida

15 .... You Raise Me Up

Audio arrangements by Peter Deneff

To access audio visit:
www.halleonard.com/mylibrary

Enter Code
7942-4533-7052-2815

ISBN 978-1-5400-0457-4

HAL•LEONARD®

7777 W. BLUEMOUND RD. P.O. BOX 13819 MILWAUKEE, WI 53213

Visit Hal Leonard Online at
www.halleonard.com

ALL OF ME

KEYBOARD PERCUSSION

Words and Music by JOHN STEPHENS
and TOBY GAD

CAN YOU FEEL THE LOVE TONIGHT

from THE LION KING

KEYBOARD PERCUSSION

Music by ELTON JOHN
Lyrics by TIM RICE

CAN'T HELP FALLING IN LOVE

from the Paramount Picture BLUE HAWAII

KEYBOARD PERCUSSION

Words and Music by GEORGE DAVID WEISS,
HUGO PERETTI and LUIGI CREATORE

EVERMORE
from BEAUTY AND THE BEAST

KEYBOARD PERCUSSION

Music by ALAN MENKEN
Lyrics by TIM RICE

HALLELUJAH

KEYBOARD PERCUSSION

Words and Music by
LEONARD COHEN

HAPPY

from DESPICABLE ME 2

KEYBOARD PERCUSSION

Words and Music by
PHARRELL WILLIAMS

HEY, SOUL SISTER

KEYBOARD PERCUSSION

Words and Music by PAT MONAHAN,
ESPEN LIND and AMUND BJORKLUND

I GOTTA FEELING

KEYBOARD PERCUSSION

Words and Music by WILL ADAMS,
ALLAN PINEDA, JAIME GOMEZ,
STACY FERGUSON, DAVID GUETTA
and FREDERIC RIESTERER

I'M YOURS

KEYBOARD PERCUSSION

Words and Music by
JASON MRAZ

LAVA
from LAVA

KEYBOARD PERCUSSION

Words and Music by
JAMES FORD MURPHY

MY HEART WILL GO ON
(Love Theme From 'Titanic')
from the Paramount and Twentieth Century Fox Motion Picture TITANIC

KEYBOARD PERCUSSION

Music by JAMES HORNER
Lyric by WILL JENNINGS

ROLLING IN THE DEEP

KEYBOARD PERCUSSION

Words and Music by ADELE ADKINS
and PAUL EPWORTH

VIVA LA VIDA

KEYBOARD PERCUSSION

Words and Music by GUY BERRYMAN,
JON BUCKLAND, WILL CHAMPION
and CHRIS MARTIN

YOU RAISE ME UP

KEYBOARD PERCUSSION

Words and Music by BRENDAN GRAHAM
and ROLF LOVLAND